#Hashtag Lightie

Lynette Linton

TEAM
ANGELICA

Published November 2017 by Team Angelica Publishing,
an imprint of Angelica Entertainments Ltd

Team Angelica Publishing
51 Coningham Road
London W12 8BS

www.teamangelica.com

A CIP catalogue record for this book is available from
the British Library

ISBN 978-0-9955162-6-7

Printed and bound by Lightning Source

Credits:

Written by Lynette Linton
Directed by Rikki Beadle-Blair
Produced by Daniel M. Bailey

Cast:

Devon Anderson as Aaron
Grace Cookey-Gam as Melissa
Adele James as Ella
Sophia Leonie as Aimee
John Omole as Bradley
Jamie Richards as David

Sound: Tristan Parkes
Lighting: Sam House
Design: Rikki Beadle-Blair
Stage Manager: Anna Sheard
Assistant Director: Gino Ricardo Green
Video Tech: Black Apron Entertainment
Dramaturg: John R. Gordon
Production Manager: Heather Doole
Marketing Consultant: Aaron Wright
PR: Laura Horton
Book cover design: Daniel M. Bailey

A Black Apron Entertainment Production

Writer/Producer

Lynette Linton

Lynette Linton is a director and playwright. She trained on the StoneCrabs Young Directors Course where she was also awarded the Jack Petchy award. Linton was nominated for a Stage Debut Award for Best Director. She is co-founder of production company Black Apron Entertainment and the current resident assistant director at the Donmar Warehouse. Linton is a former associate director at the Gate Theatre, where she directed *Assata Taught Me* by Kalungi Ssebandeke in May 2017.

Writing credits include: *Step* (rehearsed reading, and school tour, Theatre Royal Stratford East); *Service* (Boom Festival, Bush Theatre); *Chicken Palace* (Theatre Royal Stratford East), which she also co-directed; and *Ergo Sum* (Theatre Deli).

Directing credits include: *Indenture* (Dark Horse Festival); *Assata: She Who Struggles* (5 minute play at The Young Vic); *Naked* (Vault Festival 2015); *Pornado* (Theatre Royal Stratford East); *This Wide Night* (Albany Theatre); and co-director on *Chicken Palace* (R&D, and full show, Theatre Royal Stratford East). As assistant director: *Gutted* (Theatre Royal Stratford East); *Image of An Unknown Young Woman* and *The Christians* (Gate Theatre); Live Lunch's *A View from the Moon*, and *Torn* (Royal Court).

Director/Designer

Rikki Beadle-Blair

 Named fourth in this year's Rainbow List of the UK's hundred most influential LGBT+ people, Rikki is a writer, director, composer, choreographer, designer, producer and performer. He has won many awards including the Sony Award, and the Los Angeles Outfest Screenwriting and Outstanding Achievement awards. In 2016 he was made an MBE (Member of the British Empire). His many projects include feature films and TV series, including as screenwriter *Blackbird* (starring Oscar-winner Mo'nique), *Stonewall* (BBC Films) and *Noah's Arc* (MTV LOGO). He wrote and directed *Metrosexuality* for Channel 4; and feature films *FIT*, *FREE*, *KickOff* and *Bashment* for his own company, Team Angelica.

Rikki is one of the creative directors of the Visionary Youth Project for young European film activists. He also works extensively in theatre and has written 28 plays in the last decade that have been performed at Theatre Royal Stratford East, the Bush Theatre, the Soho Theatre, the Tristan Bates Theatre and the Contact Theatre in Manchester. He is a committed mentor to many writers, actors, composers and directors.

You can contact Rikki at rikki@teamangelica.com.

Cast (in alphabetical order)

Devon Anderson

Devon is best known for his roles as **Billie Jackson** in *EastEnders*; Taj Lewis in the CBBC sitcom *Kerching!* and **Sonny Valentine** in **Channel 4**'s *Hollyoaks*. Most recently he played Shahid in *Sinbad* (SKY). He has numerous other television credits to his name, and in theatre he has worked at the National Theatre, Theatre Royal Stratford East and the Lyric Hammersmith. He also worked as a presenter on CBBC.

Grace Cookey-Gam

Grace trained at the City Lit, graduating in 2013. Recent work includes Viv in *Di and Viv and Rose* (Stephen Joseph Theatre & New Vic), Agnes in *The Awakening* (Brockley Jack), Ottalan in MGM TV pilot *Dawn, Tyrant* (Fox TV) and *Justice League* (Warner Bros). She is also a busy voiceover artist and singer, with a music degree from Birmingham University. She regularly reads for the Liars League and was a BBC Radio Drama Norman Beaton Fellowship semi-finalist in 2015. @CookeyGGrace www.rebeccasingermanagement.com

Adele James

Adele is a South London born actress and writer. She has trained in acting for stage and screen at various leading independent institutions since she was a teenager, and in 2015 she graduated from the University of Bristol with a degree in Drama: Theatre, Film and Television. Previous theatre credits include: *#Hashtag Lightie* (The Arcola), *In The Pink* (The Courtyard Theatre), *Expectations* (Theatre N16). Previous Film & TV credits include: *Acceptable Damage* (2017), *Red Light* (2017), *That's What She Said* (2017), *Who I Am* (2016).

Sophia Leonie

Sophia Leonie is an actress and writer from London who trained at East 15 Acting School. Sophia recently guest-starred in BBC's *Doctors*, and has also acted in the BBC's flagship medical drama *Casualty* and Channel 4's acclaimed drama *Topboy*. Feature film credits include British Independent Film nominee *Dreams of a Life* acting alongside Zawe Ashton, and the film *Amina*, co-starring Wil Johnson and Vincent Regan. Sophia also writes a successful lifestyle blog on culture and identity, which can be found at: Sophiandstuff.com.

John Omole

John trained at Rose Bruford drama school. Since graduating he has had roles on Channel 4's *Hollyoaks* and worked extensively in theatre, including shows at Theatre Royal Stratford East, Theatre 503, and with the Thelmas Theatre Group. He has also just filmed series two of the award-winning E4 show *Chewing Gum.*

Jamie Richards

Jamie trained at The Oxford School of Drama. Credits: Theatre: Narrator in *Our Town*, Pegasus Theatre, Oxford; Wolf/Cinderella's Prince in *Into the Woods*, The Theatre Chipping Norton; Franz/ Spitz in *Kasimir and Karoline*, BAC; Thomas in *The Abattoir Pages*, The Old Abattoir; Chas in *A Karaoke Wedding*, The Union Theatre; Hugh in *Joking Apart*, The Union Theatre and David *in #Hashtag Lightie*, at The Arcola earlier this year. Film: Nick in *Sleeper: A Vampire Movie*, Catsby Films. TV: Richard Gardiner in *Luther*, BBC; and Paul Iverson *in What Remains*, BBC. Jamie is delighted to be reprising the role of David in *#Hashtag Lightie*. Twitter @Jam_Richards

Sound

Tristan Parkes has composed, designed sound and musically directed material for film, theatre, major events and television for over a decade. This includes over fifteen productions for Hull Truck Theatre, multiple productions for the Edinburgh Festival, including *An Audience with Jimmy Saville*, starring Alistair McGowan, over a decade of productions for The National Youth Theatre of Great Britain, most recently their 60th Anniversary Gala at the Shaftesbury Theatre in the West End. Tristan was a musical director on the Beijing and London Olympic Games and a composer for the British Pavilion at the World Expo in Shanghai.

Film work includes *To All The Girls I've Loved Before* (Channel 4 Films), *When Romeo Met Juliet* (BBC) and *Anna Karenina* (Working Title).

His most recent work includes a national tour of *Dead Sheep* by Jonathan Maitland, *Goat Song* (London Contemporary Dance), *Frankenstein Revelations* (Theatre Mill), *Dr Jekyll and Mr Hyde* (Blackeyed Theatre), *Zigger Zagger* (NYT) and *#Hashtag Lightie* (Arcola Theatre).

Tristan is an Education Associate for the Donmar Warehouse and Lyric Hammersmith theatres, a lecturer in Performing Arts at the University of East London and regularly facilitates music and theatre workshops across the country.

Lighting

Sam House studied Lighting Design and Production Electrics at the Royal Academy of Dramatic Art, graduating in 2015.

As Lighting Designer his theatre credits include: *The Boy, the Bees and the Blizzard* (Shoreditch Town Hall), *Scouse: A Comedy of Terrors* (Grand Central Hall, Liverpool), *The Bright and Bold Design* (George Bernard Shaw Theatre)

As Production Electrician his theatre credits include: *Suzy Storck* (Gate Theatre), *The Terrible Infants* (Wiltons Music Hall) and *Dirty Rotten Scoundrels* (Bernie Grant Arts Centre).

Stage Manager

Anna Sheard trained at the Royal Welsh College of Music and Drama. As Stage Manager credits include; *Thebes Land* (Arcola Theatre), *Pixel Dust/Wondr* (Metta Theatre), *Twilight: Los Angeles 1992, Assata Taught Me, I Call My Brothers* (Gate Theatre), *Upper Cut* (W14 Productions, Southwark Playhouse), *Sweet Charity* (NYMT, Leicester Curve), *Danny the Champion of the World* (London Contemporary Theatre, UK Tour), *Lizzie Siddal* (Peter Huntley Productions, Arcola Theatre).

As Deputy Stage Manager credits include; *House/Amongst the Reeds* (Clean Break, Yard Theatre), *The Buskers Opera* (Park Theatre), *Lotty's War* (Yvonne Arnaud, UK Tour), *An Incident at the Border* (Finborough Theatre/Trafalgar Studios 2).

As Assistant Stage Manager, credits include; *The Importance of Being Earnest* (Royal Opera House, Barbican Theatre), *Alice's Adventures in Wonderland* (Opera Holland Park), *Dancing at Lughnasa* (Theatre by the Lake), *Spamalot* (ATG, Playhouse Theatre), *Farragut North* (Southwark Playhouse).

Assistant Director

Gino Ricardo Green is a London-based director/assistant director and writer, who has worked within theatre and film from his early teens. His first assistant director job was at Hampstead Theatre for their production of *Lilies in Suez*. He is also one third of the theatre/film production company Black Apron Entertainment.

As a director Gino's 2016 short film *A Silent Night* was supported by BFI Future Film and was selected for Academy Award qualifying festival Urbanworld in New York. Most recently Gino worked as first assistant director on *Whirlpool*, a short film for *Vogue Italia*, and is assistant director for *#Hashtag Lightie* at the Arcola Theatre.

*

Producer

Daniel M. Bailey is a London-based producer, director and writer who has been working within the creative industries since his teenage years. Daniel's first step towards film and theatre was as a writer, when his short film *The Boxer* was picked up after winning a borough-wide writing competition. The short film was later presented as part of the London Olympic Games' 2012 artistic contribution.

As one third of emerging film and theatre production company Black Apron Entertainment, Daniel has gone on to direct and produce a number of short film projects such as *All is Good* by Alex Theo, *A Silent Night* by Gino Ricardo Green and a selection of other short films. As a film director Daniel is currently in post production with refreshing London comedy *Chicken Shop*. Daniel makes his debut as a theatre producer with Lynette Linton's *#Hashtag Lightie*.

Dramaturg/Publisher

John R Gordon is a multi-award-winning novelist, playwright, screenwriter and writers' mentor. With Rikki he runs the Angelic Tales new writing festival, and is co-founder of radical queer imprint Team Angelica Publishing. He wrote for groundbreaking black gay TV series *Noah's Arc* (Logo/ Viacom), and his spin-off screenplay earned him an NAACP Image Award nomination. He is the creator of the HIV-awareness graphic novella *Yemi & Femi's Fun Night Out*, several thousand copies of which were given away free at black gay clubs and venues. His plays have been performed at the Gate, the Bush, the Tristan Bates and Theatre 503. He is the author of six novels, the most recent of which, *Souljah*, was nominated for a Lambda Best Novel award, and is currently completing his seventh, *Drapetomania*, an epic tale of same-sex love in slavery times. John can be reached at john@teamangelica.com

Production Manager

Heather Doole is a freelance production manager. Her previous credits include: *Heroine* (HighTide & Theatre Clwyd); HighTide Festival 2017; *Origins Festival* (Border Crossings); *Becoming* (Donmar Warehouse Rehearsal Studio); *Assata Taught Me*, *The Convert*, *I Call My Brothers*, *Diary of a Madman*, *The Iphigenia Quartet* (Gate Theatre); deputy production manager on *Up Next! (*National Theatre); *Platinum*, *Giving*, *The Argument*, *The Meeting*, *36 Phone-Calls*, *Sunspots*, *Deluge*, *Deposit*, *Elephants, State Red* (Hamp-stead Theatre Downstairs); *Carmen* (Blackheath Halls); *No Villain* (Trafalgar Studios and Old Red Lion); *Radiant Vermin* (59E59, New York, Soho Theatre, London, and Tobacco Factory, Bristol); *All or Nothing* (The Vaults); *Firebird* and *Kiss Me* (both at Hampstead Theatre Downstairs and Trafalgar Studios); *4000 Days* and *Grounded* (Park Theatre); *Four Min-utes Twelve Seconds* (Trafalgar Studios); *The Session* (Soho Theatre); *Octagon* (Arcola Theatre); *And Then Came the Nightjars* (Bristol Old Vic Studio and Theatre 503); *Valhalla, Animals, Cinderella and the Beanstalk* (Theatre 503); *Women Centre Stage Festival* (NT Temporary Space and Hampstead Theatre). She assisted on *Bull* (Young Vic).

Thanks to:

Theatre Royal Stratford East, Gate Theatre, Unity Theatre Trust, Arts Council England, Leyton Sixth Form College, Team Angelica, Dope Vision London, John Martin, Kwaku Kyei, Maia Clarke, Arcola Theatre, Nick Connaughton, Natasha Brown, Richard Lambert and Kara M. Tyler.

Thank you to our fundraiser performers: Dane Baptiste, Magical Bones, Juliet Okotie, Alex Theo, Jordan Thomas, Mina West, and Aphek Events.

Lynette, Rikki and Black Apron Entertainment would especially like to thank everyone who took part in the *#Hashtag Lightie* development workshops, and attended and contribut-ed to our fundraiser.

#Hashtag Lightie was first performed at the Arcola Theatre 31st January – 4th February 2017. It was nominated for the Alfred Fagon Audience Award.

Black Apron Entertainment is an emerging London-based film and theatre production company. Comprising creative trio Daniel Bailey, Lynette Linton and Gino Ricardo Green, the company was established in 2014, when the trio decided to combine and pursue their creative endeavours.

They have delivered a collection of short films, music videos and other film pieces. Their 'Creativity Has No Limits' mantra is the main driver behind their recent successes, such as their first independent theatre production *#Hashtag Lightie* and short film *A Silent Night*.

Foreword

Thank you to everyone who has supported *#Hashtag Lightie* and its development over the last couple of years. I am so glad we have been able to finally share this story. Shout out to my mentors Rikki and John for running focus groups, giving advice and developing the script with me from the beginning. Big love to the cast, Adele, Devon, Grace, Jamie, John and Sophia, who bring the Miller family alive in such a nuanced, caring and brilliant way. But special, special thanks has to go to my bros Daniel and Gino who I run Black Apron Entertainment with. I wouldn't have been able to do this without you both and your belief in the project. I will never forget how many hours you have put into this. I love you both so much and can't wait to see what we continue to make together. (Also shout out to Michael Jackson just because he is the KING!)

Lynette Linton

Lynette Linton

#Hashtag Lightie

CAST

MELISSA – *mixed race, oldest of the siblings, 40. Editor. David's girlfriend.*

AIMEE – *mixed race, middle sister. 25. Unemployed. Bradley's fiancée.*

ELLA – *mixed race, youngest sister. 16 years old. At school and has her own popular YouTube channel called #lightie.*

AARON – *mixed race. The only male sibling. 25. Aimee's twin. Father of Mia. Has nerve damage to his wrist, and may sometimes wear a wrist brace.*

DAVID – *white, 38, Melissa's boss. Melissa's boyfriend.*

BRADLEY – *black, 27, Works in engineering. Aimee's fiancé.*

Online characters:

STEPH – *performance poet. Played by actor who plays Aimee.*

'D' – *vlogger, played by actor who plays Aaron.*

'G' – *vlogger, played by actor who plays Bradley.*

LIGHTSKIN BOY – *mixed race, handsome, 20s. Played by actor playing Aaron.*

COMMENTS – *performed by members of the cast or video content.*

STAGING

There is a screen upstage that becomes visible when needed. The rest of the set is up to the director. The scenes weave in and out of each other seamlessly as if happening on top of each other. There should be different lighting states to represent online and reality.

ACT I

Scene 1

Ella is recording herself at home, and her image flashes up on the screen. She is always more confident on camera than in real life.

YouTube or online comments can be shouted by other actors or recorded and played on the screen.

ELLA: *(nervous)* People! My name is Ella, and I'm here to entertain you! Okay... um... *(knocks over the camera)* Er... yeah... Everyone has been telling me for ages to start a make up vlog, so here it is... I'm giving myself over to the internet. Over to all you lot out there! I want to see people like me online! Brap, brap. *(coughs)* I'm claiming a place for the mixed race face! Eww... I don't like that... *(pause as she adjusts the camera in relation to her face)* You see this *(points at her face)* I will use it as a blank canvas for the sake of you lot...

AARON: *(O.S.)*: Who you talking to in there?

ELLA: NO ONE!

AARON: *(O.S.)* Yo Ella, come and clean up this make up shit from in front the TV man. Why can't you keep your crap in your own room? What is wrong with you girl?

ELLA: SHUT UP AARON!

AARON: All man is trying to do is watch the football –

ELLA: WHY ARE YOU STILL TALKING FOR? I'm filming something –

She turns back to the camera.

ELLA: Where was I? Yes... er... I will prod and poke and see what make up works all for my followers. I'm selfless really, it's all for you lot and nothing for me! *(pause)* Well apart from hopefully becoming a YouTube sensation... Oh and, if you want me to try out your make up on behalf of your company... you know sponsorship and that... I'm talking to you Maybelline, Bobbi Brown, Chanel, Mac... maybe even Gucci – I know that's not make up but – your girl could do with a handbag – We all know you lot give out free samples... holla at your girl. You won't regret it! This smile... will sell millions!

YouTube/Twitter comments are displayed while Ella dances. Music plays.

COMMENT: You're so beautiful Ella!

COMMENT: Look at your hair!

COMMENT: Obviously Ella gets what she wants – #team lightie...

COMMENT: She's already got more likes on Insta than any darkskin girls...

COMMENT: #lightskin girls only.

COMMENT: #lightskin don't talk to me unless you're a certain shade...

3

COMMENT: Mixed race girls are so beautiful. Just like you Ella.

COMMENT: I wish I was mixed race...

COMMENT: Loving your videos Ella! You're so pretty.

COMMENT: How do you get your hair like that? What products are you using?

COMMENT: Where are you from again? Like country-wise? Cos you're so beautiful.

COMMENT: Your make up tips are the best!

COMMENT: You're a pretty lightie...

COMMENT: You should call your channel #lightie.

COMMENT: I'm feeling that! #lightie!

COMMENT: #lightie!

COMMENT: #lightie!

COMMENT: Hashtagggggg LIGHTTIEEE!

During these comments Ella puts on more make up, including fake eyelashes. The music gets louder, Ella gains more confidence and then turns back to the camera/audience.

ELLA: Wa'gwarn lightie lovers! Keep that foundation light yet even, so you don't get blotches that appear in certain lights... make sure you have matched it fully to your skin tone. Blend it in! That's important. Same for all you darker girls! Get the right shade! This one is called 'sunset'. And remember to apply the eyeshadow with your finger, because it's not chalky and you get that nice smooth effect. You see? *(pause)* Your baby girl's got you. Shout out to all the peeps that keep sending me make up and that... I told you I would make it look pennngg... eyebrows on fleek! Pengness complete! Send me your snaps so I can see you too! I might even post you on my Instagram, and you might look as good as me. Though I have been told I have been blessed with naturally extra-long eyelashes! *(pause)* Shout out to Kimye for the samples! And thank you for all your love on my Insta, 25,000 followers in a week! I see each and every one of you! My pics look boom innit! *(pause)* Hit that subscribe button if you like my videos, and make sure you comment. HASHTAG LIGHTIE!!!

Scene 2

Aimee, Aaron and Melissa, David and Bradley come on from opposite sides of the stage holding champagne glasses. They talk among themselves.

ELLA: Personal video alert! You been asking about my family... so here they are!

The lights change. Aimee, Aaron, Melissa, David and Bradley all turn to the audience. Smiles appear on their faces. Ella runs around as if reporting for the video. They appear on the screen.

ELLA: My sistren Aimee is getting married! Woohooo!

Music plays in the background. The camera turns on Aimee. Aimee shows the ring.

AIMEE: Beautiful innit? *(singing)* He liked it so much he put a ring on it!

ELLA: *(to audience, camera on Bradley)* This is her fiancé, Bradley.

BRADLEY: She's trapped me. I'm officially Mister Aimee.

The camera turns to Ella.

ELLA: I am so excited! It's the biggest thing to happen in our famo for ages.

AARON: *(under his breath)* So your niece was no big deal then? What type of foolishness –

The camera turns on Aaron and he cracks a smile, acting cool.

AARON: Yoooo...

ELLA: Meet my big bro Aaron...

Aaron waves awkwardly.

ELLA: Aaron has the most adorable baby girl, Mia. She looks a bit like me don't she?

AARON: Er – Not really –

ELLA: He's hard you know... and he's very protective over me so all you lot out there, beware of my big brother...

Aaron strikes a macho pose.

ELLA: He even fucked up his hand once in a fight –

AARON: You should have seen the other guy! *(muttering and looking at himself in the camera)* How many people will watch this though, cos man needs a trim.

ELLA: And back to the Jay-Z and Beyoncé of Leytonstone!

The camera turns back to Aimee, who stands awkwardly with Bradley.

AIMEE: We've been together for six months.

Melissa coughs at 'six months', and Aimee's smiles flickers.

BRADLEY: Six WHOLE months... I wanted to propose after six SECONDS. When you know, you know, you know? And this is real. I mean look at her. *(to camera)* Ain't she beautiful? I finally got myself my very own caramel queen...

Melissa coughs again. David is drinking champagne.

ELLA: *(rounding on Melissa)* So when are you two getting married?

The lights focus on Melissa and David. They step forward with fake smiles.

MELISSA: Um – well –

DAVID: We don't really believe in the institution of marriage... I think it can be quite –

She nudges him.

DAVID: *(coughing)* But, this wedding – it's just the most fantastic news.

MELISSA: Aimee and er –

AIMEE: Bradley –

MELISSA: Bradley... are made for each other... it will be a extraordinary wedding.

Ella puts the camera right up into David's face, who is fake smiling. Camera back on Ella. A beat.

AIMEE: I'd like to propose a toast – well, make a speech really. *(pause as she looks at Bradley)* I have never been so happy... with life. I wasn't sure if I would ever find love –

MELISSA: *(mutters)* At 25, that must have been a major concern for you –

AIMEE: *(talking over)* But look at me now... One minute my man was standing next to me, and then suddenly he was on bended knee –

BRADLEY: Aw... my baby is a poet. *(pause)* You know man just thought... why let go of such a beautiful thing?

AARON: That was before you met the rest of us though, innit, bro.

They all laugh.

DAVID: *(to Bradley)* Run for the hills while still you can!

He laughs at his joke. They all look at him. It's not funny.

AIMEE: And I can't wait to become his wife in two weeks' time!

MELISSA: You're getting married in two weeks??? Why so quickly?

A beat. Camera on Melissa.

AIMEE: You know why. We want Mum there.

ELLA: Yeah. Right. *(She turns the camera away)* Tell us how you're feeling Melissa... how does it feel to be maid of honour?

MELISSA: I haven't been asked yet. *(pause)* I didn't think the first time I would meet my sister's fiancé would be on camera –

AIMEE: *(talking over the top)* It's just so exciting –

ELLA: *(turning camera on herself)* Hashtag exciting! And of course, what you're all waiting to hear, I'm obviously gunna be a bridesmaid! I'll post all the pictures! There may even be a Kim Kardashian style video.

Bradley laughs.

AIMEE: Elllllaaa!

ELLA: *(realises)* Eww... that's disgusting! *(pause)* I meant her wedding video – shut up...

Camera back on Melissa.

MELISSA: How many followers do you have Ella?

AIMEE: I thought this video was supposed to be about me and Bradley – tell the story Bradley...

BRADLEY: I first saw Aimee when she –

Melissa gets a book out of her bag.

ELLA: Why are you holding that, Melissa?

Melissa pushes the book at the camera.

MELISSA: This groundbreaking book we've just published? Well –

ELLA: No one is interested in a book –

BRADLEY: I first saw Aimee in the ethnic aisle of Lidl –

DAVID: Currently in the top ten of the official Bookseller charts!

AIMEE: So my fiancé and I –

BRADLEY: No one is listening Aimes...

Lights go out as the video cuts and then back up and Ella is standing in the middle of the stage.

ELLA: How cute are my sisters and their boos? *(laughs)* Did you notice the concealer Aimee was wearing? I told ya'll to get it, cos my sister has got some huge bags usually, and after I worked my magic she looked nearly as good as me... haha joke *(whispers)* I'm not joking... So there's gunna be a wedding! And soon! I'll take some pictures in my outfit cos you know your girl is gunna look fire in a bridesmaid dress. *(poses)* I may even catch the flowers and be next. The lucky man could be one of you... *(points out to audience)* I'm shouting you out @bigmanlykD, with all your wedding proposals. Keep them coming! *(pause)* But yeah, your baby girl has gotta go, cos us youngers have got school in the early hours. I'm tired yo! Snap me so I can see you too! It ain't all about me... Or is it? *(pause)* If you like what you're seeing, make sure you subscribe. Catch up with my life on Insta, what I'm doing, what I'm wearing, what I'm eating. Peace out you beautiful lot! Hashtag Lightie.

Scene 3

Lights up on Melissa and David walking into David's flat late at night. They are a little tipsy. David has an award in his hand and is reciting his award speech.

DAVID: As soon as I was given the manuscript for 'Mogadishu Burning'... I knew this was something special...

Melissa cheers and claps in excitement.

MELISSA: Do the next bit! Do the next bit!

DAVID: It took a while for others to see what I – what we – saw, but it is heartening that such a fantastic universal story about one young Somalian soldier's journey –

MELISSA: Somali –

DAVID: ...has reached so many individuals... I am incredibly proud of the work we do at Patterson Publishing, and now that I am –

MELISSA: Editor in chief –

DAVID: Editor in chief – I assure you, there is a great more to come. This one is for –

MELISSA: Diversity.

DAVID: Diversity.

MELISSA: IT WAS A BRILLIANT SPEECH BABE! Brilliant! I was so proud of you.

DAVID: WE ARE ON THE MAP!

MELISSA: And what a great book to win with...

DAVID: We are on fire baby!

He kisses her.

MELISSA: Finally... all those raw, vanguard stories... we can just publish them ourselves because you run the whole company.

DAVID: Yes I do. I run the whole fucking company.

Melissa gets up and wraps her arms around David's neck. She kisses his neck.

MELISSA: We're a power couple...

DAVID: I have been waiting to get you to myself all night...
   give you the award you deserve...

He turns his face so he is kissing her. She breaks it off.

MELISSA: I've been waiting to give you something too...

She kisses him seductively, then gets up slowly.

DAVID: Nothing can be better than your bum in that dress.

MELISSA: Mmm... I thought you might like it.

She spins.

DAVID: Might look a little better on the floor though...

He gets up to come towards her.

MELISSA: Wait... don't you want your surprise?

She pushes him back and kisses him. He sits back down.

MELISSA: Close your eyes.

David leans back and closes his eyes. Melissa goes over to her bag and takes out a manuscript. She positions herself really close to his face.

MELISSA: Open!

David does, and goes to kiss her, then notices the manuscript.

MELISSA: It chronicles the life of a young British mixed race
   girl –

He looks at her. Opens his mouth. Closes it again.

MELISSA: I can't wait to hear what you think... I mean, listen to this bit...

DAVID: *(looking annoyed)* We're really going to do this now?

Melissa starts reading.

DAVID: Okay... okay... We're doing it...

MELISSA: *(reading)* 'I don't even remember what was said, what triggered it – that moment where the one difference that, up until then, had seemed so much less important than who had a snub nose or buck teeth, who was chubby or scrawny, who had straight hair or curls – when suddenly that one, particular difference opened up a chasm between me and every other child in the classroom. The floor fell away. And I felt suddenly, utterly, cripplingly alone.'

A beat.

DAVID: *(frustrated)* Well... that was... something.

She looks at him sternly.

DAVID: I promise. I will read it. Tomorrow. *(he kisses her)* In an hour... *(he kisses her)* In five minutes. *(he kisses her and she laughs)* Well, maybe in a little more than five minutes....

He kisses her again. Lights fade.

Scene 4

Aaron comes on in front of them and starts watching TV. Aimee gets down on the floor and begins doing some leg exercises. She is exercising to Drake's 'Worst Behaviour'. Aaron gets annoyed and turns the music down.

AARON: Aimee, move man!

AIMEE: Why should I? It's my living room!

AARON: Er nah, it's Mum's living room, which means it's a quarter mine. *(pause – mumbling to himself)* At least this time you opened the window... always exercising up in here, sweating up the place like man ain't trying to watch the TV...

AIMEE: Just go home Aaron.

AARON: I am home –

AIMEE: I mean your current home – with your baby mama –

AARON: Her name is Julie.

AIMEE: Did I say I didn't know her name?

AARON: You can't be jealous of me anymore – you're doing it the right way! Even if it is a bit fast!

AIMEE: Jealous of you? *(throws a cushion at him)*

AARON: Since the womb. Since man's ten seconds younger. Since man got the better hair...

AIMEE: Better hair? You're mad... *(pause)* Can you believe it Aaron? Remember when we used to talk about you giving me away...

AARON: Do you still want me to?

AIMEE: A deal is a deal. *(pause)* I wouldn't have it any other way, bro.

They smile at each other.

AIMEE: You were joking right? Like... you don't actually think we're going too fast, do you?

AARON: If he's the one then it's fine right? *(pause)* And you want Mumsie there. That's important.

AIMEE: Yeah, it is. I want her to see me in my dress... *(pause)* And I want Mia to be a flower girl – I want you in matching outfits...

AARON: You idiot. *(pause)* I better give Bradley the big brother talk...

AIMEE: Don't do what you did with Delroy...

AARON: What? We just had a heart to heart...

AIMEE: He moved back to Jamaica, Aaron.

Bradley comes in.

BRADLEY: Wagwan twinlets. Future wife, future bro in law.

AARON: Be my guest at trying to watch the football – can't see anything with this one's big forehead in the way –

BRADLEY: Who's playing?

Aimee looks at him sharply.

BRADLEY: *(as if rehearsed)* Not that I care about the football... because I'm here to start planning our wedding... I'm so gassed...

AIMEE: I know you are. Did you bring your scrapbook?

AARON: Scrapbook? You got a wedding scrapbook, bruv?

BRADLEY: Aimee! *(turns to Aaron, his voice gets quieter as he speaks)* My mum collected a couple of wedding artefacts over the years... I saved it for her... it's gunna be handy now innit...

AIMEE: *(mutters)* Is that the story we're telling people?

AARON: As long as you tell me what time and where the church is I'm all good. Anyway, big bro talk pending fam – gotta make sure you're the right guy for my twin ain't I? Because if you hurt her...

Aaron puts on his serious face then cracks a big smile.

AARON: I'm kidding bro –

BRADLEY: To be honest, man was more scared for you...

AARON: I'm gonna ignore that comment as I am a father and will not be enticed into violence... Later, big head!

Aaron leaves.

BRADLEY: Babe. Who do you think would win in a fight, me or Aaron?

Aimee smiles and changes position. Bradley watches her.

AIMEE: Don't forget Melissa's arranged for you to 'bond' with David tonight...

BRADLEY: Ahh, yeah...

AIMEE: Try and have fun... he's a bit dry. Good luck.

Bradley takes his scrapbook out of his bag.

BRADLEY: So... I picked out some napkin patterns for us to think about. I marked them out for you. I also highlighted the different flower choices.

AIMEE: Okay... just pick one. I trust you.

BRADLEY: Aimee... I've chosen everything so far... don't you care? It's a very important choice.

AIMEE: It's bloody napkins... people won't even notice them once the curry goat comes out. *(pause)* You know we can't afford much, we all chipped in for Mum's dream cruise.

BRADLEY: Well, that's what credit cards are for!

AIMEE: Be careful – I want it to be simple – not a big fuss – just a nice dress and some food –

BRADLEY: Baby, it has to be special – I want to spoil you. You're my beautiful, exotic, Irish, Bajan queen. I want you to have everything you want.

AIMEE: I already do. *(she kisses him)* Now let me carry on working out. I've only got ten days, and I got a wedding dress to fit into boy...

Aimee turns over and stretches.

BRADLEY: Jeez... *(sings in the style of Rihanna)* Wild, wild, wild thoughts!

Aimee does a twerk for him, laughing. Bradley goes to shut the window.

BRADLEY: Why you got this open for? You not felt how cold it is? That's your Irish side coming out you know.

Aimee frowns. Bradley closes the window.

BRADLEY: I'm joking – you know – it's cold in Ireland innit? You can't feel it because you're from there... that's the joke...

AIMEE: *(mutters)* How would you know? The furthest you travelled is the end of the Central Line.

BRADLEY: Well it ain't rocket science is it? Do you want me to help you stretch or something?

He positions himself over her awkwardly. She lets him take her leg and help.

BRADLEY: *(looking at her)* How the hell did I get you? *(pause)*

You know our yutes are going to be so cute with their part Irish selves. They're going to be sweet little caramel tings.

He looks at her intently. Ella comes on. She stands in front of Aimee and Bradley. She begins talking as the lights fade down on them, and does her make up.

ELLA: Wa'gwarn lightie lovers! I know you lot are feeling my concealer and yeah, you're right, I do have the best skin tone. Just add a bit of powder blush... and I used a blue eyeliner on my waterline. Just makes it a bit more dramatic... *(pause)* Oh my days! A picture of me as a child has been posted on a mixed race appreciation page. Shout out to @smithy2000 for your comments! I was cute innit? *(pause)* If you wanna see more pictures of the cutest children ever, then type, 'cute mixed race kids' into Facebook, and like my friend's mixed race baby page... See you later lightie lovers! HASHTAG LIGHTIE!

Ella switches off the channel and receives an email. She opens it. The actress playing Aimee comes on as Steph, on her spoken word channel 'Speak Like Steph'. She begins to click her fingers.

STEPH: It's time to for us to talk/Put down your iPhones, iPads, exit Snapchat and the gram/ look me straight in the eyes for a whole five seconds/ because it's time we took a walk. Let's start with the topic that gets us all riled/ sees us reviled/ let us/ respond to the tough question that is never but should be at the forefronts of our minds/ The indoctrination that gets us distracted by surfaces. Women of colour, this is not the time to look away, this is the time to stand together and ask/ Why are we pulling each other apart, using melanin/ and curl and coil/ as weapons in this fight we did not start/ it hurts and tears at every beat of my heart/ Malcolm X said we're the most disrespected, neglected and unprotected, yet we cling on to the boundaries that keep us disconnected/ you need to stop and ask yourself who really is in control? Cos I refuse to add ammunition to this war/ I will not maintain this man-made sink-hole.

Ella switches the video off annoyed.

ELLA: Lonnnnnng...

She picks up her phone and posts a picture on Instagram.

ELLA: *(to herself)* Take a look at this instead.

A picture of Ella posing flashes behind with the slogan 'If she ain't exotic, she ain't a topic'. She watches the 'likes' go up rapidly.

ELLA: *(to herself)* Hashtag Lightie!

Scene 5

Melissa comes on during this and begins setting the table. This makes Ella stop and turn off the camera. She is less confident now. Aimee comes in sits at the table. There is silence for a while. Aaron comes in and Ella perks up.

ELLA: Dinner selfie?

She poses for a picture with Aaron. He makes a funny face. It flashes on the screen.

21

MELISSA: *(to Ella as she kisses her cheek)* How was school, lil' sistren?

ELLA: *(not interested)* Fine.

MELISSA: I was thinking of joining Twitter...

Ella looks up, horrified.

ELLA: You? Why? For what?

MELISSA: How about 'Snap Chat'?

AARON: Mia ain't going online until she is at least 18 —

ELLA: I'm on it and I'm not 18 —

AARON: Exactly and look how it's damaged you. *(he ruffles her hair)* And before you say anything Mel, I'll bring Mia over tomorrow... she's been asking to see her aunties...

MELISSA: Good. *(pause)* I saw a great spoken word artist online recently — I sent you the link Ella — did you watch? See if I had Snapchat I could snap it to you —

ELLA: You're so embarrassing —

AARON: It's true. You are.

MELISSA: But you love me, don't you? *(pause as she notices Ella's eyelashes)* Are you wearing fake eyelashes Ella? I told you... they're going to pull out your real ones.

ELLA: I don't actually wear them —

MELISSA: You have them on –

ELLA: I was demonstrating how to –

MELISSA: Don't blame me when your eyes are bald and you have to wear those yard brushes permanently.

AIMEE: So I was thinking –

MELISSA: There is a woman at work who actually lost all her eyelashes and it took years for them to grow back. YEARS Ella.

AIMEE: With such a quick turnaround to the wedding, Bradley and I would appreciate some help – you know taking pictures, sorting out music and that –

AARON: Yeah I'm in –

ELLA: Sounds good to me.

Silence. They look at Melissa.

MELISSA: So... Bradley. Does he live at home – with his parents?

ELLA: Here we go...

MELISSA: What does he do?

AARON: He's an engineer, innit?

AIMEE: Don't question me about Bradley, Melissa.

23

ELLA: *(talking over)* Anyone want a glass of juice?

MELISSA: I'm just trying to get to know more about –

AIMEE: You obviously have a problem with my life partner.

ELLA: *(talking over)* I would like some juice...

AARON: *(to Ella)* I'll have some...

MELISSA: *(sniggers)* Life partner?

ELLA: *(talking over)* Just pouring myself some juice...

AIMEE: Fucking drink your juice then Ella!

AARON: You don't need to take it out on Ella, Aimes.

AIMEE: *(to Melissa)* Spit it out then. What's the issue?

MELISSA: There's no issue. *(pause)* Six months – How well do you know him?

AIMEE: I love him.

MELISSA: This is the rest of your life-

AIMEE: So Aaron can have a baby after ten seconds –

AARON: Yo. Don't bring me into this. I ain't got no problem with you and your dude, man.

ELLA: They looked pretty cute in my video Melissa.

MELISSA: Just live with him a couple of years – you've never even lived alone –

AIMEE: So?

MELISSA: And why does the wedding have to be so fast?

AIMEE: Melissa. We don't know how long Mum has left, and I want her there! *(pause)* I want her to get back and it all be ready: she doesn't have to do anything except be there on the day. Otherwise you know she'll get caught up in stressing over every detail and she doesn't need that. I don't want her to get ill again.

AARON: She won't get ill again, Aimes.

A beat.

MELISSA: But then why can't you have a long engagement? Take your time... let him get to know Mum and the rest of us...

AIMEE: Aw. I see. I get it. I know what this is about.

MELISSA: What?

AIMEE: You're jealous.

Silence.

ELLA: Oh shit...

MELISSA: Excuse me?

AIMEE: Your 25-year-old sister is getting married... and your 25-year-old brother has a child. It's your worst nightmare. It should be you... you're the oldest by a long shot...

MELISSA: David and I don't believe in patriarchal structure –

Lights change – spotlight on Ella as she talks to her video. She is still sitting at the table. She is more confident when she is on camera.

ELLA: People always ask me... 'Why are you always online Ella? Why don't you get some real friends?' You lot out there are all the friends I need.

Lights change – back to the dinner table. Camera off.

AARON: Mel ain't that old –

MELISSA: Gee, thanks.

AIMEE: I am trying to work out what your issue is with Bradley.

Silence for a few seconds.

MELISSA: 'Caramel queen'?

AIMEE: Now you're just looking for something to be angry about –

MELISSA: I just think –

AIMEE: Why the fuck does any of that matter?

MELISSA: Don't swear at me. It doesn't matter. I don't care. Go and marry him... be happy. Just don't let him treat you like some kind of trophy.

AIMEE: Trophy?

MELISSA: *(laughing)* I'm not arguing you with you Aimee – I just want to make sure he sees you for you – not just –

Melissa's laughter angers Aimee.

AIMEE: You're the biggest hypocrite I've ever met.

MELISSA: Excuse me?

AIMEE: You're going out with your boss Melissa! And we all know why – and you sit there –

MELISSA: David being promoted has got nothing to do with our relationship –

AARON: You lot need to calm down man!

AIMEE: He is a complete and utter idiot. And don't act like you haven't said it too Aaron. We all hate him! *(to Melissa)* That's why you hate Bradley innit? He reminds you of what you can't reach... you've settled.

MELISSA: 'Settled?'

AARON: I don't actually hate him Mel – I just think –

AIMEE: You're so desperate, and yet you sit there trying to preach to the rest of us how to fucking live. Look at your own guy before you come cussing mine –

27

Bradley and David fall in through the door, drunk, singing 'Drunk in Love'.

DAVID: Wa'gwan bredrens and sistrens! We're home!

David walks over to Melissa and leans on her in his drunken state.

BRADLEY: *(to Aimee)* Hey babay. You look sexy.

AIMEE: You look drunk.

ELLA: At 7 pm...

BRADLEY: *(laughing)* I love you Aimee... you're my caramel queen... and I actually really like David.

DAVID: Woooohooo! A Miller that likes me!

ELLA: He ain't a Miller yet.

DAVID: You Ella, need to stop being so negative, and smile occasionally. You look like you're plotting to kill me and post it on the YouTube.

Bradley laughs.

AARON: That is funny... and it would probably get so many views.

Ella looks at the audience. Lights change again: camera is on.

ELLA: They don't take me seriously. When I am in Hollywood and Kylie Jenner's BFF they will really see how special I am.

Lights change as she snaps out of her video as she hears what David said.

DAVID: Well, more views than the engagement video... have you guys seen that yet? *(stroking Melissa's face)* Bradley... look... I told you the comments were bullshit... she is black... I told him I only go out with black women...

MELISSA: *(outraged)* Excuse me? Where has that come from?

BRADLEY: I never said she wasn't black... she's just not black black cos she's mixed innit. *(turns to Aimee)* Not like you babe. You're now officially black black cos you're with me.

AARON: 'Black black'?

MELISSA: 'Black black'?

AIMEE: What the fuck is 'black black'?

BRADLEY: Language, language...

DAVID: You're so beautiful.

MELISSA: What are you talking about?!

DAVID: You. And me. And you. And me. And Brad. Who is a legend by the way. *(pause)* Hold on... Why is Aimee black but Melissa isn't Brad?

They all look at Bradley.

BRADLEY: I didn't say that, *I* didn't say that... That's what people were saying on the comments underneath Ella's video, not me...

AIMEE: Ella's video?

BRADLEY: Yaaaaa... the one of all of us!

MELISSA: Why are we even having this conversation?

AARON: We're all black.

BRADLEY: Ahhh... so you call yourself black then?

AARON: What do you mean 'call' myself?

BRADLEY: Well – you know – cos you lot are Irish too innit. Is 'black' like a short cut?

MELISSA: A short cut? A SHORT CUT TO WHAT?

DAVID: *(laughs with Bradley)* We were in the pub, and I said to Brad, 'Have you seen it?' and he said 'No' and we watched it...

AARON: I don't call myself anything. I'm just what I am.

BRADLEY: I didn't say you weren't –

DAVID: And you should see what people were commenting on it...

AARON: I'm black. Not Irish.

BRADLEY: But –

AARON*: (jumping up, angry)* NOT. IRISH.

Aaron slams his bad fist on the table. He winces.

AIMEE: Aaron...

A beat. Bradley laughs, clearly not realising how angry Aaron is.

AIMEE: *(to Bradley)* Don't laugh at him!

DAVID: Okay... well, what would you say Aaron's daughter is –

AARON: What?

MELISSA: David –

DAVID: Considering she has a white mother and all that –

AARON: So?

BRADLEY: Well she is – white – we've all seen her. You had a baby with a white woman, which means your baby is basically white – I mean you could say quarter caste –

AIMEE: Quarter caste?

BRADLEY: Doesn't Mia have blonde hair?

They look at Aaron. He opens his mouth and says nothing.

MELISSA: *(pointing at Bradley)* And this is the man you want to spend the rest of your life with, Aimee?

DAVID: I mean Mia is still black – well partly, isn't she? Her grandmother is fully black, she's never going to escape that.

ELLA: Escape?

MELISSA: Escape?

AIMEE: *(to Melissa)* Look what you've settled for –

AARON: *(to Bradley)* My daughter's ethnicity is none of your business fam.

BRADLEY: Nah – obviously not – but I was just commenting on what people will say...

DAVID: Like in the engagement video.

AIMEE: Why do you keep going on about the damn video?

DAVID: Watch it for yourself...

The lights change and comments are heard/seen.

COMMENT: So you got one white sister and one black sister then?

COMMENT: How can one of your sisters be with a black man, and the other one with a white dude? Weren't you lot raised in the same family?

COMMENT: Well it's clear to see who feels closer to their white side innit.

COMMENT: She didn't look like the type of bitch to go for a nigga ya know.

COMMENT: She didn't look like the type of lightie to go for a cracker.

COMMENT: Someone is a white man's whore...

COMMENT: Someone is a black man's bitch...

COMMENT: When a mixed race girl chooses her man she chooses her side.

Lights change back.

BRADLEY: That's what I meant when I said that she wasn't 'black black'.

Scene 6

Ella's channel rings out. Ella gets up, comes forward and talks to the audience. She picks up a wedding magazine.

ELLA: Wa'gwarn lightie lovers! These have taken over my yard. My future bro in law got excited and left these clapped airy fairy magazines all over the place. *(pause as she opens the magazine)* Oooh I like her, she's lightskinned, like me... She's hot. *(shows the camera)* Anyway, my sistern continues to scatter them around like I wanna see these women squeeze into dresses that she ain't ever gunna afford. £12,000 for a dress you're only going to wear once? *(pause)* And you know my mumsie doesn't even know yet... so that's going to be a whole other ting when she gets back innit? *(pause)* I'm gunna be relying on you lot to keep me going, cos I'm proper stressed already. *(pause as she sees more comments: she reads them out loud)* 'You pathetic ugly hater #bitch #confused #fuckedupfamily'. Er... look, yeah... don't send me hate on my channel... especially about my famo. This right here, ain't about that. SO FUCK YOU! Don't make me say it again. *(pause)*

MELISSA: *(offstage)* Ella! You ready for me?

Melissa comes on smiling. For a second Ella looks like she wants to talk about the hating with her. Big difference between on and off camera.

MELISSA: You okay sweetie?

ELLA: Yeah... yeah... I'm fine. Let me just finish the rest of this bit... *(she turns back to the camera)* One good thing is I now get to experiment with wedding make up – have a look and post your favourite wedding styles and I'll see which one I want to recreate. Sorry Team Darkskin, I only specialise in a certain shade. It's all love though. So I'm going to show you how to do some make up using my very own model, you lot all know my sister Melissa...

MELISSA: Hi guys....

ELLA: But before we get started on this, make sure you click that subscribe button and hit me up... Remember to catch up with my life on Instagram, what I'm doing, what I'm wearing, what I'm eating – Today I will be giving my sister what I like to call a 'caramel twist' look.

MELISSA: *(confused)* A what twist what look?

Ella pushes her back and begins doing the make up.

ELLA: Make sure you always rub the shimmer in... not too dark, but not too light either. Just right.

Comments appear again.

COMMENT: She's a basic lightie, would still fuck her over a blick chick though...

COMMENT: All lighties are emotional wrecks... Ella is literally the only one I can tolerate you know.

COMMENT: She's hitting over ten thousand views!

COMMENT: Pengers!

COMMENT: Buff!

COMMENT: Choong!

COMMENT: Ain't that the sister that's with the white guy? What a waste... She has got a BACKKKOOOFFFFF!!!!

COMMENT: That family is so fucked up...

COMMENT: I beg you educate yourself about history before you try and come with your 'blended family'.

ELLA: Hashtag Team Lightie...

A snap of Melissa and Ella is projected onto the screen as the music from the next scene begins to play – 'Who's That Lightie?' by Ramzee. Ella watches the next scene.

Scene 7

The actors playing Bradley and Aaron come on as D and G, two early 20 year olds. They are filming a YouTube video.

G: Welcome back to our channel!! I'm 'G'.

35

D: I'm 'D'.

G: We're here to talk about this whole light skin, dark skin debate... because it's all over Black Twitter innit, it dominates that shit –

D: Basically, there has been a long history of debate, anger and contempt between darker skinned people and light skinned people...

G: I hear it's common in the Asian community too... wa'gwan all my Bangladeshi, Pakistani, Sri Lankan *(pause as he thinks)* Kashmir, Indonesian, Indian beauties... I see you...

D looks at G in disbelief.

D: Anyway... it's getting worse, because lighties – light skinned black and mixed race girls – are waste. So we're gunna call out some of them who are doing their ting on YouTube, Twitter, Facebook, Insta, Snapchat...

G: ...Tinder, Flickr, Myspace, hifive, yeah man said hifive don't act like you don't remember that shit... I just wanna call out that hashtag lightie chick, what's her name? Ellie, Ellen, Eleanor, Elisa...

D: Ella blud.

G: Who thinks she's all peng. She's a typical example of who we're talking about... how old are you girl? Calm down...

D: Yeah but you've being preeing her for time. Don't act like you're not desperate fam. You were sending her wedding proposals and everything. She shouted you out, fam! Big man like D!

G: I told you that wasn't me blud! My bro hacking my account and shit... But this is what I'm talking about fam! Obvi she's a peng ting – cos she's a lightie – but she's the stooshiest thing on road – did she ever reply though? And look at her make up videos, and all that stuff about her peng lightie sisters... who cares? Do I care? Just because you're a little bit peng does not mean that man cares if your sister is getting married. Or what your middle name is... why do I need to see that shit? *(pause)* SHUT YOUR CHANNEL DOWN BLUD!

D: We know there's bare mandem have gassed all you lighties up. I know there's bare celebrities that gass you lot up too. But we are here, because it's time that the mandem finally see the truth.

G: I remember in 2006 when Kanye West said: 'If it wasn't for race mixing there would be no video girls. Me and most of our friends like mutts a lot.' Did you hear what he called you?

D: Mutts...

G: Mutts...

G notices that D is sweating.

G: Ooookkkay... Some of you lighties are pretty, but you lot think you can destroy man's life with one flick of your extra long eyelashes... it ain't cool.

D: I actually hate you all you know... I'm done with you all.

G: Every lightie who joins Instagram expects at least 5000 followers before she's even uploaded a picture.

D: If you text a lightie in January and she texts you back before Christmas you is lucky bro.

G: A lightie can walk past me and man can smell the 4565 unread DMs on her phone...

D: They're probably all from you though bruv...

G: Everyone needs to learn some history –

D: Like in *Roots* and *Django*...

G: Being light didn't make you better back then –

D: You lot were just the ones that got caught!

Scene 8

Comments begin to flood the screen.

COMMENT: Truth!!!!

COMMENT: Shut the channel down!

COMMENT: Those boys chat so much shit.

COMMENT: How about you all actually just open a book for once?

COMMENT: That Hashtag Lightie girl is just a stupid bitch! I'm with D and G!

Ella comes centre-stage and looks up at the comments. She faces the audience.

ELLA: So I'm going to do the 'Mixed Girl tag' stream. Thanks for tagging me @exotic67. Basically, I answer some set questions and then anything you've sent in truthfully and live. *(reads)* 'What is my favourite colour?' *(pause)* I would say... beige... I mean, isn't that obvious? *(pause)* 'Favourite restaurant?' Now I know you lot are expecting me to say Nando's or something but I'm a little bit more classier than that you know... I mean look at me... so it will have to be a TGI Friday ting! Yeahhhh boooiii! Give me one of those burgers and I am all goooodd... and that Jack Daniels chicken ting! When I pick a man... he better take me there for dinner every night. *(pause)* Thank you to those two fools who shouted me out! You know you actually doubled my subscribers! And how many have you got? Ten? Let's compare numbers one day yeah? *(pause, she breathes and then smiles)* 'What's my heritage?'

Lights out on Ella and she freezes. Aimee and Bradley are stage right, awkwardly staring out front. They are holding champagne.

BRADLEY: *(addressing one of the audience)* That's great. So tasty... and moist... you know when you eat a cake and it's just not moist? No, we both felt that this cake was just right... we loved the marzipan roses, didn't we babe?

Aimee nods.

BRADLEY: And the champagne... I think this is the right choice... not breaking the bank but not too cheap.

He takes a sip.

AIMEE: Don't you think you had enough of that last night?

Bradley swallows loudly.

BRADLEY: Er – yeah – you're probably right. *(to audience)* We – er – I think we will definitely go with this Caribbean Dream package sir –

AIMEE: We'll think about it.

Bradley looks alarmed.

BRADLEY: Could you give us a few seconds? *(smiles)* Thanks... thanks... wedding jitters...

Aimee doesn't look at him. He sighs.

BRADLEY: Sorry we got drunk last night. Sorry I like David. Sorry I pissed off your brother and sorry your sister hates me and... what else do I need to apologise for?

Aimee says nothing.

BRADLEY: Is this about the video? *(pause)* What do you think about the video – the comments and that?

AIMEE: Did it change your mind about my ethnicity again?

BRADLEY: What is that supposed to mean?

AIMEE: *(Turns back to audience)* Er? Yeah... we'll try a cocktail...

Lights back to Ella.

ELLA: So my mum is from Barbados, and my dad was from

Ireland. He died just before I was born. *(reads and answers)* Nah, I've never been to Ireland, but I've been to Barbados twice. *(reads quickly so she can change the subject)* 'Do you see any benefits to being mixed race?' Er, yeah have you seen my hair? *(laughs, reads)* 'Which background do you embrace the most?'

Lights back on Aimee and Bradley.

AIMEE: One minute I'm Irish, and then 'black black'?

BRADLEY: That wasn't me that said that... it was the stupid people on the internet...

AIMEE: You said it too Bradley – *(turns to audience)* – the strongest cocktail on the menu please – yeah the Trini Carnival Dream is perfect –

BRADLEY: Yeah but I was joking babe. I'm always joking. You know me... come on...

A beat.

BRADLEY: But are you really going to tell me you don't feel more loyal to your black side? I know you...

AIMEE: 'Loyal'? This isn't a Chris Brown song! It's not up to you to tell me what I am – I get that enough from everyone who looks at me. They're always expecting us to make a choice. When I'm both!

BRADLEY: All I'm saying is, you like rice and peas more than shepherd's pie...

AIMEE: Bradley! Be serious! This is serious... look what you said to Aaron – questioning him –

BRADLEY: Baby – *(to audience)* Does this really look like the right moment to ask us what dessert we prefer?

AIMEE: *(to Bradley)* Oh really? I thought your preference was anything 'caramel'. Mixed race 'caramel tings' – like fucking trophies –

Light on Ella.

ELLA: Shout out to @firecrazeneubian who asks, 'Why is your sister with a white man? Black women shouldn't sell out.' *(pause)* Fuck that, I'm not even answering that – get a fucking life... it's no big deal.

Melissa and David enter stage left, arguing.

DAVID: What is the big deal Melissa? *(pause)* Is this about last night?

MELISSA: Urrrggghhhhh...

DAVID: Okay... It's not –

MELISSA: How far have you got with the manuscript?

DAVID: Mel – look – let's get a bottle of wine and –

MELISSA: Have you even read any of it? The one thing I asked you to do –

DAVID: *(mutters)* I wish...

MELISSA: What else have I asked for?

DAVID: Look, I know it must mean a lot to you because of the subject matter –

MELISSA: So you have read it?

DAVID: Just because you're the only ethnic minority in the office doesn't mean that you have to keep pushing this constantly, Melissa.

MELISSA: I'm sorry?

DAVID: Sorry – half ethnic.

A beat. Light on Ella.

ELLA: My sister isn't choosing anything. I mean, I like all different types of boys, and if I ended up with a Latino, does that mean I'm choosing to be Latino? That doesn't even make sense.

Lights on Aimee and Bradley. Bradley pulls her away from the audience.

BRADLEY: Trophy? What the fuck? Why do you lot always care about what other people think, man?

AIMEE: 'You lot?' One second you're calling me black, then Irish, and then next it's 'you lot' yeah? You can't even make up your mind what Aaron should call himself. Why should you choose what I am?

BRADLEY: *(rolls eyes)* Do we have to have this conversation here, Aimee?

43

AIMEE: Yes. We do. *(pause)* I ain't got no problem with just being me – and then suddenly –

Lights back to Ella.

ELLA: *(reading)* 'What's it like being a half breed?'

Ella looks shocked. She opens her mouth and then closes it. Lights on Bradley and Aimee.

BRADLEY: Why the fuck do you care? Why let them –

AIMEE: It's like everyone chooses what I am... and now you're doing it! You've always been doing it. Do you even realise?

BRADLEY: Doing what? Loving you? Acknowledging your beauty?

AIMEE: No Bradley, defining me. *(pause)* You don't walk into a room and people anticipate where you're from, what fucking side you chose.

BRADLEY: What do you think people see when I walk into a room? You not noticed you're engaged to a black man?

AIMEE: Which apparently means I'm a black woman. So what if I turned to you right now and said I felt more white? Huh? Would you wanna marry me then? *(pause)* Is there no space for that side of me in your world?

BRADLEY: Oh, I see – I thought this was supposed to be 'our' world. But this right here is only about your struggle innit... next you'll be coming out with Twelve Years A Lightie.

AIMEE: That's not funny!

BRADLEY: You know what is funny? *(pause)* I didn't see how self absorbed you were Aimee.

AIMEE: Self absorbed? Who the fuck are you right now?

BRADLEY: I'm late for work. *(to audience)* We'll be in contact about payment and such.

He leaves.

AIMEE: Actually, I would rather cancel the booking.

Lights on Ella.

ELLA: 'How old is my niece?'

Lights flick to Aaron, standing alone at the side of the stage.

AARON: Yeah... oh sorry, I thought they were finishing early today. *(pause)* No? Well, it's okay... I'll wait. *(He checks his phone)* I'm here to collect my daughter. Yes. She's in this class. *(pause)* Well I ain't seen YOU before. *(pause)* My girlfriend normally picks her up as I have work... look, why am I explaining myself to you? *(pause)* I just said... I am here to collect my daughter. What is this? I don't see you questioning anyone else. *(he looks around as he realises what's happening)* Oh...

Lights flick to Ella.

ELLA: 'What's my favourite book?'

Lights on Melissa and David.

DAVID: I think you take a lot of this on your shoulders and you don't have to.

MELISSA: Someone has to publish unheard British minority stories. Like Walter Tull... have you even heard of him?

DAVID: Melissa – not tonight please –

MELISSA: You saw the comments on Ella's blog! How ignorant people are.

DAVID: I did. I saw. But –

MELISSA: Well maybe we can actually make a difference –

DAVID: Melissa –

MELISSA: I mean, what about Marie Stopes? I can't believe we published another book on her last year...

DAVID: She was the godmother of family planning –

MELISSA: She also wanted all mixed race people sterilised at birth to stop them experiencing the 'horror of being neither black nor white.' Don't you think that is something people should know about?

DAVID: Why? Why do people need to know that? That's just depressing and doesn't help anyone today. I think people need to be educated but we need to do it the right way...

MELISSA: History, literature, is the right way –

DAVID: Yeah, well, once you're responsible for the whole budget you begin to look at things a bit differently.

A beat.

DAVID: You're upset about the video.

MELISSA: David, you're not hearing me...

DAVID: Personally, I don't get what the big deal is with all this mixed race stuff – Aaron really overreacted yesterday... and how did he hurt his arm?

MELISSA: I don't think Aaron overreacted.

DAVID: Do you want to be called black? Like him? Because if you do then that's okay... I mean, mixed race is basically black isn't it? I mean, isn't there all that – all that one drop rule stuff –

MELISSA: I didn't realise you identified with slave owners.

DAVID: Well, let's call you mixed race then and that's good too because that means you're half of me –

MELISSA: Excuse me?

DAVID: I'm trying to understand, Mel... I do understand. I see how men look at me when I'm with you... I notice it too.

MELISSA: What?

DAVID: The man with the dreadlocks at the bus stop last week. That white man at the award ceremony.

A beat.

DAVID: I just think we should talk about how you're feeling –
properly, because you obviously have issues about your
identity –

MELISSA: I can't believe you're saying this...

DAVID: And I can help you through them – through this –

Melissa takes the manuscript out of her bag.

MELISSA: What did you think of the manuscript?

DAVID: I'm opening a bottle of wine.

MELISSA: Answer me, David –

DAVID: I haven't finished it yet – but it's good –

MELISSA: Which bit? *(pause)* Which bit are you up to?

DAVID: The bit with the census – chapter three.

*Melissa opens the book at chapter three and reads. She gets
emotional.*

MELISSA: 'I stared at the census form looking for myself.
White. Black Caribbean. Black African. Black other. Indian.
Pakistani. Bangladeshi. Chinese. Any other ethnic group.
They didn't give me an identity. Any. Other. Ethnic. Group.
I wasn't worthy of a box.' *(pause)* Did you know that was
only in 1991? That we didn't have a box to tick in 1991?

DAVID: Melissa, what is wrong with you? Why are you –

MELISSA: Patterson needs to step up and publish something worthwhile for once!

DAVID: What about 'Mogadishu Burning'? *(pause)* Patterson has been your livelihood for years – it's where we met –

MELISSA: And now you're running it!

DAVID: So is this why you're fucking me then? To further some sort of pro-black agenda?

Melissa is so shocked she doesn't know what to say to him.

MELISSA: Goodbye David.

Lights flick to Aaron.

AARON: Why is that so hard to believe? Ain't you seen a mixed race child before? *(pause)* Don't patronise me blud. You know what, I need to take her home now... this second. We have somewhere to be. Can you get her for me please? *(pause)* I don't care if the class ain't finished. I'm her father, and this is an emergency. Get her for me now. Please. *(pause)* Well go call the head teacher then. I'm taking my daughter home... I'm not losing my temper... DID YOU NOT HEAR ME SAY PLEASE? *(pause)* Well go and get my daughter then. Cos I'll go into that class and take her out myself. Watch me! *(starts to go in)* MIA! *(looking for her)* MIA AIMEE MILLER GET. HERE. NOW! What do you need me to do? Show you her fucking birth certificate? Show you my blood so you can see it's the same colour? Maybe do a fucking paternity test? Is that what you need to me do? Fuck this. What the fuck are you looking at? *(the nursery bell rings, and children begin coming out as the staff try to escort him away)* Don't touch me bruv! MIAAA!

Lights back on Ella, getting emotional as she reads more Twitter messages.

ELLA: 'Your mum sold out too. She's a white man's whore... I bet your brother only goes for white girls – he looks like the type.' *(pause)* 'Why do you think you're so pretty? You're not. And stop hating on darker girls.' *(pause)* When did I ever hate on anyone? Stop asking me your nasty racist questions yeah? Stop sending me those light skin parody videos! Leave me alone! This isn't fun anymore.

She jumps up in anger, but is distracted by the next scene as...

Scene 9

The actor playing Aaron comes on as LIGHTSKIN BOY on Youtube. He begins to film a video. He appears on the screen.

LIGHTSKIN BOY: *(American accent)* Shout out to all my followers... I know ya'll are loving my pictures. Lightskin brothas be like...

Drake's 'From Time' begins to play. Aaron walks around the stage nodding his head to the beat. He begins to mime when the first set of lyrics, sung by Jhené Aiko's, kick in. This carries on to the beginning of Drake's first line, when it cuts.

LIGHTSKIN BOY: Let me take a selfie.... *(takes three with different poses)* This is so much work... the lighting in this room isn't doing it for me... I'ma have to use a filter or some shit. *(takes another picture)* just one more... just one more... hashtag cute, hashtag sexy, hashtag teamlightie.

'Lightskin' memes begin to appear on the screen behind him. Lightskin Boy's phone rings. He answers.

LIGHTSKIN BOY: Baby, don't get mad at me... you know I love you... you know you got my heart. You know I know I can be your hero baby. You know I can take away the pain...

He puts the phone down and takes another selfie. His phone rings again. He answers.

LIGHTSKIN BOY: Yoooo, dude. Yeah man... yeah tell her to come round. You know nothing is going to happen. We'll mostly watch a nice film... and cry. You know how I do. *(pause)* The park? Nah, I can't be sitting out in the sun for long periods of time my brotha... I don't wanna catch no tan. Aww I gotta go... it's time for me to – yo it doesn't matter if I'm late bro, I'm lightskinned.

He turns to the audience and breaks character.

LIGHTSKIN BOY: Thanks for watching my videos. You know I'm just playing... Send this to anyone you think suffers from the lightskin problem today! Let's get them sorted out! Oh and shout out to that #lightie girl. Keep your family's business offline.

He slinks offstage.

Scene 10

A new Ella video pops onto the screen.

ELLA: Yo, I don't know where all this random hating has suddenly come from but I don't do this YouTube stuff so I can get cussed. None of you actually know me, so you don't know if I'm stoosh do you? Let me just let you know though, if you did come and try and chirpse me – yeah you – you know who I'm talking about – you would get straight

51

up rejected... and you know what, I'm just gunna come out and say it, because you lot are calling me a hater so come I spread a little hate... It ain't my fault that you ain't as pretty as me. It ain't my fault that you feel inferior, it's not my fault that no-one likes pasty bitches or 'dark chocolate'. I'm sick of everyone who is like one shade darker than me giving me a screw face like I disrespected every black woman by simply existing. I'm just talking truth bitches. Oh you know what, if you wanna look like me get a torch and shine some light on yourself. *(shines a light on her face)* Maybe then people might actually see you in your pictures. Stop talking about my sisters and their men yeah... TRUTH... *(pause)* Back to business. Tomorrow, we will be talking about make up tips for festival season. And also, make sure you catch me at my YouTube meet and greet next week. Can't wait to see you all. Hashtag lightie.

Scene 11

The scene cuts as if the video got cut off as Melissa runs into the living room, talking on her phone. She is carrying loads of papers. Aaron is sitting watching the football.

MELISSA: Yes – no I'm not at home, I'm at my mother's... but I can quickly use my sister's tablet.

She switches on Ella's tablet, and begins shuffling through her papers.

MELISSA: I can assure you this is the book we want – no I haven't spoken to David Ross. Well actually, I have – No I'm not trying to go over his head... *(pause)* Listen, this tablet is just loading up. Let me call you back when it's done, and we can go through it? Good. Give me five minutes.

Aimee comes in, sees Melissa and Aaron and rolls her eyes.

AIMEE: Why do the two of you keep forgetting that YOU DON'T LIVE HERE?

AARON: I can't hear you – the football is on –

AIMEE: Lying around here all day every day –

 AARON: I can't hear you – the football is on –

Melissa and Aimee look at each other.

AIMEE: Where's Ella?

MELISSA: She isn't back from school yet. *(pause)* Did you take a look at the comments – the ones that they were talking about.

A few seconds.

AIMEE: Yeah – yeah I did.

MELISSA: There's pictures, insults and parody videos. What is all this? I feel so old.

AIMEE: Mmm... you're right – you're old.

MELISSA: You're still going to argue with me? After this?

AIMEE: You didn't have to get rude to Bradley like that last night, Mel –

MELISSA: You were rude to David –

AARON: Am I actually hearing this correctly?

AIMEE: I thought you couldn't hear.

AARON: 'Hi', 'How are you?' 'How was your day?' How about you actually ask that to each other? It's always you two going at it all the time. For fuck sake... and now you're sticking up for your men. Both of them idiots.

Silence.

MELISSA: How are you Aaron?

AARON: Not great.

Silence.

MELISSA: Where is Mia?

Silence.

AIMEE: Where is she? Aaron –

AARON: Oh, my fucking 'white' daughter, who I can't pick up because I'm black?

MELISSA: Aaron –

AARON: That's what they saw at her school. That's what they see when I'm getting pulled over by the police. That's what they all see. I'm a black man. A 'black black' man.

MELISSA: I'm sorry Aaron. That's outrageous! I'll write a letter to the school –

AIMEE: You want me to go down there and punch someone? I was born a whole ten seconds before you... I suppose I should stick up for you once in a while.

They smile. Melissa turns away from them and begins tapping around on the tablet.

MELISSA: What the hell is this?

Ella's YouTube and Twitter account automatically logs on as Melissa fiddles. #Lightie begins to flash up continuously, a louder noise each time one pops up on the screen.

Ella runs onstage. The other siblings fade into the background. The comments below flash up on the screen, the voices either recorded or live. If live, we shouldn't see the performers' faces. Ella reacts to the screen. Each comment gets more angry.

COMMENT: Ella! Are you that fucking stupid? And racist? Who's been hating on you?

ELLA: I didn't mean you –

COMMENT: This lightie thinks she's a pengers you know – someone needs to put her in her place –

COMMENT: Wake the fuck up!

ELLA: Listen, it was the comments I was getting – I'm sorry –

COMMENT: You're not sorry – you don't care about anyone but yourself Ella.

ELLA: What?

COMMENT: It's true – all you do is let them guys gas you up.

ELLA: You're just jealous...

COMMENT: Jealous of what? You ain't even that hot mate.

ELLA: LEAVE ME ALONE!

COMMENT: I should have known about you – I coulda just looked at you and known – lighties are pretty to look at but are all fucked up in the head.

ELLA: What did you just say?

COMMENT: You heard me 'hashtag lightie'.

ELLA: STOP IT!

The voices get louder. Ella begins to scream and shout, distressed. A knife comes out. Her face is cut. She runs off-stage. The sound of the comments gets louder and louder and takes over the space completely. Lights change to match this.

COMMENT: Hashtag lightie...

COMMENT: Hashtag lightie...

COMMENT: Hashtag lightie...

ALL: Hashtag Lightie...

Blackout.

Scene 12

Lights up. Ella, Aimee, Melissa and Aaron are in a hospital room. Ella's face is bandaged up.

AIMEE: At least it didn't damage a nerve.

MELISSA: And you only have a couple of stitches.

Silence.

AARON: Ella, who did this to you?

MELISSA: Why didn't you talk to us sweetie?

AARON: I could have done something...

ELLA: I wanna go home –

AIMEE: Why didn't you let us help –

ELLA: Because you lot are the reason this happened!

Silence for a few seconds.

ELLA: As soon as I put that stupid engagement video up the comments all changed...

Ella is really crying now.

ELLA: They loved me before – they're just all jealous of us you know – that's what it is – they be mad hating – I mean otherwise why would they do this?

57

MELISSA: But what about what you said?

Ella looks at her.

MELISSA: You need to take some responsibility.

ELLA: It's jealousy – they want 300,000 views – they want the fame, the followers, and the life of –

AARON: The life of a hashtag lightie yeah?

AIMEE: You did say some nasty stuff Ella – is that why you didn't want to go to the police?

ELLA: You lot are too old to understand.

MELISSA: What do you mean when you say 'hashtag lightie?'

ELLA: You see... you don't even know what it means –

MELISSA: Why is that your slogan #teamlightie?

AIMEE: Most of your friends are black...

MELISSA: Our mother is black... darkskinned... where has this come from?

ELLA: I dunno – I just – it's just my name... people started calling me and I claimed it...

MELISSA: Claimed it? What has it even got to do with being mixed race?

AIMEE: It doesn't...

ELLA: It's banter...

MELISSA: Banter?? You think you can say anything because everyone does it behind the safety of a computer screen?

ELLA: 350,000 views Mel! I'm special.

Silence. Ella looks out at the audience as if looking online.

ELLA: They're my friends...

MELISSA: Friends?

Ella turns back.

ELLA: It's not my fault everyone wants to be mixed race –

MELISSA: Well it was a different world when I was growing up.

AARON: Not everything has to be a history lesson Mel...

AIMEE: And it was different for me and Aaron too. That's the thing with time, Mel... things change.

MELISSA: So now us being mixed race suddenly makes us better than everyone else, does it?

AARON: Melissa...

AIMEE: Let's not do this here...

Ella stands up.

ELLA: Didn't the doctor say I could leave now? I wanna go home.

MELISSA: Look at what's going on around you, how the media are still choosing what we should be... choosing who we are – how Leona Lewis is mixed race, but Mark Duggan is black – why do you think that's happening?

ELLA: I don't know –

MELISSA: Of course you don't... Why would your mind go beyond YouTube? Why would your mind go beyond yourself?

AIMEE: Okay. Enough. Let's go...

MELISSA: Ever thought about why are we the acceptable face of black? *(pause)* Is it because they can't yet talk about how black is beautiful so they look to someone who is closer to their skin tone? And you can stand there as a 16-year-old and champion that ideology?

AARON: That's not what she was doing –

MELISSA: You haven't given a second thought to anyone else around you, have you?

ELLA: I did –

Silence.

MELISSA: We might suddenly be fashionable in this country but only a few breaths ago I was spat on in the street... Or do the comments we used to get not count because they weren't on Twitter?

Scene 13

The lights change and voices come on as they did for the Twitter comments. They also appear on the screens. The voices reflect the different times and are in a range of accents. The actors playing Bradley and David may deliver these lines as other voices.

BRADLEY: You're dirty....

DAVID: Is your blood the same colour as ours? When you bleed, is it red?

BRADLEY: Let's find out...

DAVID: Where are you from? Like really from?

BRADLEY: Why is your hair like that? It's not a proper afro but it's not a normal hair either...

DAVID: You don't look like a typical mixed race person...

BRADLEY: Confused as fuck!

DAVID: I want cute little brown babies one day!

BRADLEY: In Kenya they call you lot 'point five'. Cos you're half.

DAVID: Half white... half black! Half caste!

BRADLEY: I think it's great that you're half caste. You get the best of both worlds don't ya? And you're pretty...

DAVID: How can your dad be white when you look like a golliwog?

BRADLEY: You act like a coconut innit...

DAVID: Race mixing is dirty.

BRADLEY: You don't fit in anywhere.

DAVID: You should relax your hair you know, cause it looks really picky right now.

BRADLEY: You act more white than black you know –

DAVID: You act more black than white you know –

BRADLEY: When you straighten your hair you look Turkish.

DAVID: When you curl your hair you look black.

BRADLEY: My mum says I can't date mongrels –

DAVID: Vain –

BRADLEY: Self-obsessed –

DAVID: If the white people drew a line in the sand you know where you're going to end up –

BRADLEY: Dad doesn't want a half caste in the house –

DAVID: 'She believes that all half castes should be sterilised at birth. Thus painlessly and in no way interfering with the individual's life...'

BRADLEY: '...the unhappy fate of he who is neither black nor white is prevented from being passed on to yet more un-born babes...'

Lights change back to the hospital.

AARON: Mel. Enough. She gets it.

MELISSA: Tell her.

ELLA: Tell me what?

MELISSA: Tell her how you really fucked up your hand.

A pause.

ELLA: His hand? What has that got to do with anything?

AARON: She knows. *(pause)* In a fight.

MELISSA: Tell her.

AARON: I – don't – I –

Aaron looks at Ella and back at Melissa, then over to Aimee. He opens his mouth but is overcome with emotion. A beat.

AARON: It's not even –

AIMEE: He got it in Ireland. The last time we went. Before you were born.

ELLA: Ireland? That happened in Ireland?

A beat.

AARON: Yeah.

AIMEE: We were attacked. The day after Dad's funeral.

ELLA: What?

A beat.

MELISSA: I told you both not to wander off! I remember... I said wait...

Ella is looking at Aaron. She touches his shoulder.

ELLA: Aaron?

A beat. It's as if Aaron is watching the scene unfold in front of him as he tells it to Ella.

AARON: We thought they were joking. Jeez, I was just happy to actually meet some Irish peeps. We even started to laugh along. *(pause)* We only clocked the levels when they started monkey noises... Aimee looked at me and then suddenly – we just ran... Didn't know where we were going...

A beat.

AARON: You know what's jokes? I still remember stupid pointless things about that day. Like how cold it was, or the smell of the fucking salt in the air *(pause)* or how everyone stared at us, fucking boring into my skin with their gaze – it's fucked... They were screaming any shit at us... And I actually stood there, letting their words engulf me...

proper baffled like – I mean, I thought we were Irish too. At least that's what Dad had told us –

AIMEE: He told us we were welcome there.

AARON: The first time he took us there, when we were really little. He said that. I remember: we were Irish too. *(pause)* But being up there, surrounded by all those yutes, that was the first time I ever felt scared. I realised that my skin meant I wasn't safe in a place that was supposedly part of me. How did that even make sense? So I shouted back and...

AIMEE: ...one of the boys grabbed me. Aaron just went for him – he went for all of them – and they – they –

A beat.

AIMEE: It musta been like twenty feet cause we were right at the top of the... and he – he landed on the – landed on the rocks. *(to Aaron)* I thought you were dead, I really did... I was – I was screaming... but they had all run off and left us there... Your arm was in the most fucked up position – I remember – it was like you were double jointed... cept the amount of blood –

MELISSA: I will never forgive myself for not being there. I should have been there.

AIMEE: Hey – it wasn't your fault Mel –

AARON: We were kids. *(pause)* You know he said he wanted to check the colour of my blood. See if we were humans –

65

AIMEE: Or half breeds...

A beat. Bradley and David rush on, worried.

BRADLEY: This hospital is like a maze... thank god we found you – fuck, Ella... are you –

AARON: She's fine. It's fine.

DAVID: Can we do anything?

Bradley grabs Aimee's hand.

AIMEE: Thank you. For coming.

Silence. Melissa and David look at each other.

BRADLEY: Okay... Let's go... We can all squeeze in my car...

Ella stands up. Bradley spuds Aaron. They all begin to move towards the door. David grabs Melissa's hand.

DAVID: I'm here. Let me drive you home. Please Melissa.

AIMEE: Go with him...

Melissa looks at Aimee then at David and nods. She waves the others off as she and David walk off together. Ella stays onstage with Aaron. They hug as she cries.

AARON: Hey, it's okay...

ELLA: I didn't know. I didn't know it was that bad for you guys.

Lights down.

Scene 14

Lights up stage right: Melissa and David are talking in his car. A beat.

MELISSA: Thank you for coming. That was kind of you.

A beat. They look at each other.

DAVID: 'You're not half anything. You're fully you.'

MELISSA: What?

DAVID: *(reading manuscript)* 'Dad's soothing Irish tone calmed my ticking brain and suddenly I could really think straight. I wasn't the one who had woken up this morning angry or perplexed about this. I wasn't confused about my parents' different skin tones. It was only after I left the house that the constant questions and negativity rained down upon me – seeping into my hair, eyes, pores, thoughts, and before I knew it, I was drenched by them, I was morphed into them – not me anymore. They were a constant puddle I kept stepping in and then, just when I thought I had escaped, I realised my shoes were still soaking...'

Pause.

DAVID: Why didn't you just tell me you wrote it?

MELISSA: I wanted your honest opinion.

DAVID: The birth of the twins was a bit of a giveaway though...

She smiles.

67

DAVID: It's extraordinary.

A beat.

DAVID: We should call it 'Beige Britain', mocking the Sun front page you mentioned.

MELISSA: I don't think we should work together anymore.

DAVID: Melissa –

MELISSA: I'm going to start my own publishing house... *(pause)* Don't look at me like that, you know it's been coming for a while.

DAVID: I –

MELISSA: It's a good thing, David. It's going to be a good thing. *(pause)* Let's see which of us publishes my manuscript first...

Melissa gets out the car. David smiles to himself and watches her go.

Ella steps forward and opens her mouth to record a video, but her confidence fails her. She steps back into the dark.

Lights up on the middle of the stage. Aaron is sitting there, reading a story to Mia.

AARON: 'And the little bird wrapped his wings around himself and melted back into his nest, closed his eyes, knowing tomorrow would be another beautiful, bright day...'

He looks down and sees she is sleeping. He looks at her for a while.

AARON: You're so beautiful, Mia. Daddy loves you. Daddy wants you to be – Daddy will protect you from...

A beat. He looks at his arm, and then back at her for a few seconds. He breaks.

AARON: Mia – daddy will protect – daddy will try – I promise I will try –

He can't finish the sentence. He sighs, closes the book, and switches off the light.

Lights change. Aimee and Bradley are stage left, talking.

BRADLEY: *(speaking really fast so he can get it all out)* Magdelia from the restaurant called. The wedding is only a few days away. I think we just need to sit down and talk... we obviously misunderstood each other. Let's have a calm, adult conversation before making any rash decisions.

A beat.

AIMEE: Do you think – do you think Ella will be okay?

BRADLEY: Of course she will. It's all going to be fine babe. I promise.

A beat.

BRADLEY: I love you...

AIMEE: Maybe you need to get to know me a bit better... as a whole. Maybe I need to get to know you some more too.

BRADLEY: So... we're not breaking up?

AIMEE: No, course not...

Bradley breathes a sigh of relief.

AIMEE: Let's just slow things down. *(pause)* A wedding in two weeks? What were we thinking?

BRADLEY: But I thought you wanted your mum there –

AIMEE: I do. And she will be. When it's right. *(pause)*

BRADLEY: But our deposit –

AIMEE: It's just money –

BRADLEY: Just money... lots of *my* money... *(Aimee looks at him)* but whatever you want babe. We can wait as long as you want. And besides, we gotta make sure we are in the right place for our future trophies... because our little ones will be trophies of not only our love –

AIMEE: Let's stop with the trophy metaphor... it's been overplayed. *(pause)* I love you.

Bradley is overwhelmed and hugs her.

AIMEE: You cheesy wasteman...

BRADLEY: *(singing)* Wild wild wild! *(pause)* You know... I am going to marry you.

Bradley smiles and kisses her.

Lights back on Ella. She is standing looking outwards. She switches the screen on.

Steph comes on. She is talking to her viewers.

STEPH: There are many ways to stand up and say what we're thinking without putting down brothers and sistas/ otherwise we're all sinking/ in this cesspit/ in this unlit/ journey of questioning. Young girl. Please don't let this hinder your voice. See this as a choice/ to learn how to dance in this worldly match, cause we can be sparring partners in our debate, push differing experiences, envelop ourselves in beauty, but do it all without spreading hate. I challenge you to challenge me. Always. But remember, we're stronger together. *(She turns to Ella, breaking the online/real world barrier)* Do you see that now Ella?

Steph reaches out as if to touch Ella just as D and G come on.

D: I warned that chick! We warned her! I need to see the video fam! Bet her Instagram ain't popping now –

G: Calm down bruv...

D: Hashtag lightie, my back foot!

Ella is getting more frustrated and angry as they talk. She touches her face, looks like she is going to cry. Tries to calm herself down.

D: She's making the whole thing up –

G: I dunno fam –

D: She just wants more likes on her now-dead channel – she's lying fam – she probably cut herself – you know what lighties are like –

A video of Ella running away bleeding pops up. In the corner, the view counts go up. D and G watch while Ella cries at the image of herself.

Scene 15

Melissa steps into the light, centre stage, holding her manuscript. The video of Ella fades out.

MELISSA: *(reading)* 'A fleeting moment. I knew my baby sister had just entered the world. I felt it. I had been walking along the coast. The same coast where I knew my little brother's defiance and my little sister's courage had shone on long after they had left the scene of the crime, and something seemed to burst alive inside my being. My body felt lighter... I was floating. I was standing in the place which had fractured my family, feeling... hope? I was no longer the half caste girl being labelled in the playground... the 'other' without a box... I was the woman who had found her place. I belonged. Because I had belonged all along. With my wispy hair, freckled face, and the birth of my baby sister, I could see my own box emerge through the questions. I took no hesitation in stepping inside. I was here to create my own definition.*(She holds the book out to Ella) We* are here to find our own definition. To find ways to say: we belong.'

Ella takes the book. Melissa leaves. Ella flicks through it. She touches her face, and bandage. She closes her eyes. She turns the camera on and her face flashes above on the screen. She pulls off her bandage slowly, tears appearing in her eyes. Her wound is apparent.

ELLA: People –

Blackout.

End.

Also available from Team Angelica Publishing

'Reasons to Live' by Rikki Beadle-Blair
'What I Learned Today' by Rikki Beadle-Blair
'Summer in London' by Rikki Beadle-Blair

'Faggamuffin' by John R Gordon
'Colour Scheme' by John R Gordon
'Souljah' by John R Gordon

'Fairytales for Lost Children' by Diriye Osman

'Black & Gay in the UK – an anthology' edited by John R
Gordon & Rikki Beadle-Blair

'More Than: the Person behind the Stereotype' – edited
by Gemma Van Praagh

'Tiny Pieces of Skull' by Roz Kaveney

'Slap' by Alexis Gregory

'Custody' by Tom Wainwright

'Fimi sílẹ̀ Forever' by Nnanna Ikpo

Lightning Source UK Ltd.
Milton Keynes UK
UKHW021517100219
336887UK00005B/209/P